Contents

P·I·T·C·H·E·R·S

Mr Duckbody, Superstar!

Caroline Pitcher

Illustrated by John Harrold

Blackie

First published 1988

British Library Cataloguing in Publication Data

Pitcher, Caroline
Mr. Duckbody, superstar !—(Pitchers).
I. Title II. Series
428.6 PR6066.I7/

ISBN 0–216–92362–X

Blackie & Son Ltd
Bishopbriggs, Glasgow G64 2NZ
7 Leicester Place, London WC2H 7BP

Printed in Great Britain by Thomson Litho Ltd,
East Kilbride, Scotland.

1

Lizards and Butterfly Cakes

Alastair had buttercream in his hair. It was all over his face, too, like gooey freckles.

He was making butterfly cakes for the school Summer Fete. Maria Nicolossi had asked him to help her with the Cake Stall. Alastair liked insects, so he was making two dozen butterfly cakes.

He mixed them up in the chip pan because it was the biggest thing he could find.

The butterfly cakes burned.

He made some gooey stuff for the tops with butter and sugar. He cut off the top of each little cake and tried to make it look like a pair of wings. He slurped a blob of gooey stuff onto each cake and wedged on the wings.

Alastair put the cakes on his father's best blue plate.

Then he put Lenny, his best lizard, in a little glass box and hurried off to school. Lenny was going to be in the Pet Show.

The playground was busy. Everybody was getting ready for the Fete. Alastair walked slowly carrying his cakes and his lizard. He was still wearing a big apron that came right down to the ground.

Mrs Wilson the Headteacher charged across the playground like a rhinoceros. The Fete must begin at two o'clock. It was going to be opened by the television star, Wayne Stag.

Mrs Wilson skidded to a halt just before she collided with Alastair.

She peered down at the blue plate and the little black lumps on it.

"What a good idea, Alastair," she said. "Home-made crisps."

She peered down into the glass box and shuddered.

Alastair frowned. They were not crisps. They were butterfly cakes.

Mrs Wilson rushed off across the playground. There was a fight among the children in Fancy Dress. A boy in a doctor's coat was trying to do a leg transplant on a smaller boy.

And there was trouble at the Pet Show. Mugwump the school cat was hissing and spitting at the other cats who had dared to come into his playground.

As soon as Mrs Wilson had gone, Darrill swaggered up.

"What are those black things?" he said.

"Butterfly cakes," said Alastair.

"They look more like Dead Moth Cakes to me," said Darrill and swaggered off.

Alastair arrived at the Cake Stall.

Maria said his butterfly cakes looked delicious. She said she liked cakes well-done.

Maria's grandmother had given her a white lace cloth to put the cakes on.

"And my father gave me cakes from the shop. Look!"

She pointed to a wooden tray with rows of sticky cakes oozing with honey. There were fruit cakes and chocolate cakes that other people had made, and there were strawberry tarts.

Alastair's mouth watered.

"Do we get free cakes, Maria?" he asked hopefully.

"No," she said. "But we get first choice. I've just decided."

Alastair gazed at the strawberry tarts.

"I'll buy them all," he said. "I can afford it. I sold a baby snake last week."

"No, Alastair. That would be greedy!" rang

out Miss Mopper's voice behind him. Miss Mopper put down a plate of Gingerbread Men with buttons and bow ties made from currants.

"You look lovely, Miss," said Maria. "You've blow-dried your hair, haven't you?" Miss Mopper's bright red curls sprang out round her head like the petals on an infant's drawing of a flower. She was wearing a new sunshine-yellow jumpsuit.

"Thank you, Maria," smiled Miss Mopper. "I did dry my hair today. I don't usually have the time . . . I can't wait to see Wayne Stag! Those strawberry tarts look delicious, I must say. Who made them?"

"Don't know, Miss. Someone had left them on the table before I arrived."

"Perhaps you could put a tart on one side for me?" whispered Miss Mopper. She looked quickly over her shoulder to see where Mrs Wilson was. Mrs Wilson was telling Mr Duckbody the Schoolkeeper where to hang the flags, over by the fence.

"I see your father has sent some Baklava, too Maria," said Miss Mopper.

"Pardon, Miss?"

"I mean the nut and honey cakes. Please

save me two of those. Err . . . what are those little . . . those sort of . . . you made those, didn't you, Alastair?"

"Yes, Miss Mopper," said Alastair proudly.

"Please save me one of those too. Ugh!" squealed Miss Mopper, suddenly. "Alastair, I don't think you'll sell many cakes if you leave your lizard on the stall."

"But it's Lenny, Miss."

"Well take Lenny over to the Pet Show where he belongs. And it's LIZARD not LYSADD . . . there, I've changed it for you. Now, where are my Bingo boys. Michael? Lennox?"

"I wish you would stay still for a minute, Miss," cried Lennox. He wobbled up in high-heeled red leather boots.

Lennox was dressed up as someone called Duke. He had seen Duke on Top of the Pops. He had borrowed a purple silk shirt from his big brother and red tights from Maria. The only boots he could find belonged to his mother. They were too long, but they were also very narrow. Lennox felt as if his feet would drop off.

His friend Michael was dressed as Superman. They would have to wear their costumes

while they ran the Bingo Stall because the Fancy Dress was not judged until half-past three.

"Stop giggling, Maria," frowned Lennox. "Just because you're not dressed up. WOW! Look at those cakes. Maria, why don't you help Michael run the Bingo and I'll run this stall? They'll go like hot cakes."

"No thank you, Lennox," said Maria firmly. She smacked Lennox's hand as it hovered over a strawberry tart.

"But it was love at first sight. Just one little strawberry tart?" pleaded Lennox.

"No! Mrs Wilson said that nobody can buy anything until Wayne Stag opens the Fete at two o'clock."

"But you'll sell them all while Lennox and I are slogging away on the Bingo," cried Michael.

"I can put one aside. I'm keeping *lots* for Miss Mopper."

Lennox and Michael stared at Miss Mopper. She went as red as the strawberries on the tarts because they had found her out.

"Right. We'll have two strawberry tarts and two nutty things and two pieces of chocolate cake and . . . "

"And two butterfly cakes," beamed Alastair, getting back just in time.

"I can't see any butterfly cakes," said Michael.

"There," said Alastair proudly, pointing at the crumbly piles with their blobs of buttercream.

Michael and Lennox peered at the piles.

"Alastair made those little cakes," explained Miss Mopper quickly as Michael and Lennox pulled faces.

"Oh. All right. We'll have two butterfly cakes as well," said Lennox sadly.

"Let's get some money from our Mums," said Michael.

Duke hobbled and Superman flew across the playground to the Plant Stall to borrow money for the cakes. Their mothers were selling spider plants and violets, and trailing red geraniums on little stands.

Alastair and Maria counted the money for the cakes carefully. Then they put the cakes on one side.

"Hurry up," said Miss Mopper. "We have a lot to do before Wayne Stag opens the Fete."

"Did you see him in last night's episode?" said Michael. "Do you think he'll find his twin brother that he hasn't seen since he was three days old?"

"Hurry UP!" cried Miss Mopper. "We have to—"

Nobody heard Miss Mopper's last words.

There was a loud crash.

Then there was a cry. And a lot of angry shouting.

2

The Flag Monster

"Look Miss," cried Alastair, jumping up and down. "Mr Duckbody is having a fight with his ladder."

On the grass by the fence lay Mr Duckbody the Schoolkeeper. He was shaking his ladder with both hands and shouting at it. Something was muffling his words.

Miss Mopper ran across the playground. The children ran after her. All except Maria. She wasn't going to leave her cakes on their own for anything. Certainly not for Mr Duckbody.

"Are you all right?" said Miss Mopper. Mr Duckbody had heaved away the ladder and was fighting with the flags that he had been putting up on the fence. One was wrapped round his mouth. A string of flags was tying up his legs.

"Mr Duckbody looks like a sort of flag monster, doesn't he, Miss?" said Alastair happily.

Miss Mopper hissed "Stop laughing" at Lennox and Michael.

Mr Duckbody staggered to his feet. He swayed as if he was drunk. Then he toppled down again because his legs were all tied up with flags.

"Hold his arms," cried Michael.

Lennox and Alastair each held one of Mr Duckbody's arms while Michael hurried round him in circles unwinding the string of flags.

"It's like unwinding the bandages from a mummy, isn't it?" said Lennox.

"Did you see what happened? DID YOU SEE?" cried Mr Duckbody when he had pulled the flag away from his mouth.

"No we missed it. We were looking the other way," said Alastair sadly.

Mr Duckbody jumped over the pile of flags and dashed across the grass.

"Ah HA!" he cried. He picked up a piece of wood and waved it around his head. Everyone backed away. Alastair thought that Mr Duckbody might hit him, so he ran back to the Cake Stall. When he got there, Maria said that the buttercream in his hair looked like dandruff. She told him to go and wash it off. Then she borrowed a clean tea-towel from the Afternoon Teas and wrapped it round Alastair's head so that his hair would dry.

Over by the fence, Mr Duckbody was still waving the piece of wood. His long black moustache was bristling at the ends.

"My ladder is broken again! This rung fell off," he cried, waving the piece of wood. "It's a different rung from last time. Now I'll have to mend it again. I've got to put up the flags, and I've got to put up the Coconut Shy, all before Wayne Stag opens the Fete. If you ask me . . ."

Lennox nearly said, "We didn't!" but decided it was a bad idea. Mr Duckbody would not have laughed.

"If you ask me, Mrs Wilson should buy me a new ladder with the money from this Fete. Never mind computers and fish tanks. Where are we without a ladder?"

"Mrs Wilson doesn't buy ladders," said Miss Mopper gently. "They come from School Supplies, Mr Duckbody, not from Headteachers."

"But they DON'T come from Supplies, Miss Mopper. I ordered a ladder two months ago. Where is it, may I ask?" Mr Duckbody sighed. "*And* I had to clean the photograph of Wayne Stag that She put in the Entrance Hall. Some little horror drew big orange ears on it, and . . . and . . . whatsits. You know, what insects have."

"Wings?" said Lennox.

"Abdomens?" said Michael.

"Thorax . . . ies?" said Lennox.

"Lots of eyes?" said Michael.

"Millions of legs?" said Lennox.

Each time Mr Duckbody shook his head.

"Antennae?" suggested Miss Mopper.

"That's them! Two enormous antennae sticking out of his head. I had to rub hard to clean them off."

"So there ANT ENNY now!" cried Lennox and he and Michael rolled on the grass laughing.

"Very witty, Lennox," smiled Mr Duckbody. "But I had to clean other things too. Oh dear me, Miss Mopper! Worse. Much worse."

There was a silence. Mr Duckbody seemed to want to tell them about the Other Things, so Miss Mopper asked, "What things, Mr Duckbody?"

"Mess, Miss Mopper, mess. It's all very well Her having a Pet Show, but dogs and cats leave mess. On the porch. In the flowerbed. Cleaning up dog mess is part of my job as well as everything else, it seems."

Mr Duckbody looked unhappy. Michael didn't blame him, and Lennox decided he wasn't going to be a Schoolkeeper when he grew up.

"I'd better go and get the tool box and mend the ladder," said Mr Duckbody. He wandered off.

"Poor Mr Duckbody. He is having an awful day," said Miss Mopper, gazing after him. "I would like to know who drew all over that photograph."

Michael looked quickly away. He knew who had drawn on the photo. It was his little sister Annie, with her face paints.

Annie had started to draw ears on everything, as if she had just noticed that people had them. And she had been looking through Michael's book about insects. That was where she saw the antennae.

The insect book had given Annie the idea for her Fancy Dress. She was a Bumble Bee. She wore Michael's old yellow and black striped football top, and Mum's black tights. They were all wrinkled around her fat little legs.

Annie's stomach was round like a bee anyway, and she had a basket on each side for the pollen. Her face was bright yellow with big black eyes. She had big yellow pompoms on the ends of pipe-cleaners for antennae.

"Come on, you two," said Miss Mopper briskly. "We must set out the cards for the Bingo. And we must collect the change from Mrs Wilson. Two pounds' worth will be enough. Hurry up. Lennox, if you can't walk in those boots then take them off. Wayne Stag will be here any second."

"My fans may not recognise me without my boots!" cried Lennox. But he stepped out of the boots and ran along carrying them. He had no socks on, just sticking plasters all down the side of his toes where the boots rubbed.

"Come on, Duke," laughed Miss Mopper. "Perhaps Superman will carry you. This Fete opens in fourteen minutes' time."

3

Wayne in Spain

"The Fete opens in thirteen minutes' time," said Mrs Wilson as they went into her room. "Except that there isn't anybody to open it."

"What do you mean?" asked Miss Mopper.

"I mean he's not here."

"Are you sure, Mrs Wilson?"

"Yes. Unless he's hiding under a chair, or crouched in the Lucky Dip."

"Don't worry," said Miss Mopper gently. "He's just a little bit late. There are thirteen more minutes."

"Twelve minutes now," said Mrs Wilson. "Hurry up, man, hurry up! Most of those people have come just to see Wayne Stag. We could make lots of money. We could buy new maths equipment. We could buy a new ruler for every child in the school. Think of that!"

Lennox thought of that, but wasn't very excited.

"Oh . . . . I hoped we could buy another

computer and a tank full of tropical fish," said Miss Mopper.

"Basics, Miss Mopper, basics!" said Mrs Wilson. "I suppose we'll have a staff meeting about it, and everyone will want to buy something different."

Mrs Wilson pointed out of the window. "See the little stage all ready with the microphone? See all the girls from the secondary school? And their mothers, aunts and grannies? They watch Wayne Stag on 'Dean Street Diary' three times a week and now they've come to watch him open our Fete this afternoon. We've had posters up about it for weeks. And now he's not here!"

"Ring him up," suggested Miss Mopper.

"That would seem bad-mannered. He is doing us a favour opening the Fete. I can't ring him up and shout 'Where do you think you are?'"

"But it's only right he should open the Fete if he used to come to this school."

"He did. Oh, before my time, of course. His real name isn't Wayne Stag, you know. It's Wilfred Birkbottle."

"Shall I ring him up and try to charm him?" smiled Miss Mopper.

"No thank you. I can charm him perfectly well myself," snapped Mrs Wilson. She snatched up the telephone.

Lennox wondered if it was a good time to tell Mrs Wilson his joke about the antennae. He decided it was not. He wondered why schools had Summer Fetes if everyone got so cross.

"My Mum says Wayne Stag has made so much money that he's bought a great big house at the other side of town," whispered Michael as Mrs Wilson dialled the number. "It costs hundreds of thousands of pounds. It's got a swimming pool, a jacuzzi and four garages. And a cinema."

"My Mum doesn't like him," whispered Lennox. "She says she would rather watch a toad dressed up."

"Quiet, you two," said Miss Mopper.

"Good afternoon," said Mrs Wilson into the 'phone. She had fixed a smile on her face and her voice sounded soft and husky.

"May I speak to Mr Stag, please? Who? Who's that? Who's this? Oh, this is Mrs Wilson, the Headteacher from Mr Stag's primary school. Oh Ha! Ha! His old primary school. He doesn't come here now, of course."

Mrs Wilson laughed with her mouth but not with her eyes. Her eyes could have turned anyone to stone.

"You see," she went on, "Mr Stag promised to open our Summer Fete this afternoon, and he hasn't arrived. How much? How much what? No, we're not paying him anything . . . what do you mean, people always pay him to open things? We're a school. We don't have any money to spare."

Mrs Wilson pulled a face at the 'phone. Then she said, "What time will he be here? It's not far. TORREMOLINOS! What do you mean, he's in Torremolinos? He promised us faithfully that he would be here. Is there anyone else there who could open a Fete? Only a budgie? What about you? Oh, you have to sweep the tennis court. I see. Yes, I could leave a message but I don't think I will. Goodbye."

Mrs Wilson put down the 'phone. "The Headteacher who was here before me was wrong about Wayne Stag," she said. The children had never seen her so angry. "She said he was the nastiest little boy she had ever met, but he might grow out of it. Well he hasn't!"

Mrs Wilson charged out of her room into the big hall. She pounded away on the piano as

if she wanted to blow the roof right off.

"How awful!" said Miss Mopper. "I suppose Wayne Stag is making lots of money in the nightclubs."

"Where is Torremolinos, Miss?" said Lennox.

"It's in Spain. People go there for holidays."

Lennox sighed. "Wayne Stag just isn't good enough for you, Miss Mopper. He sounds horrible. Isn't there anyone else famous who used to come to this school?"

"There was someone in the local paper, Miss, who used to come here," said Michael. "Len Someone . . . there was a photo too."

"You mean Len McCarthy. He's famous all right! He has been sent to prison for fifteen years."

"He wouldn't get here in time for two o'clock, then," said Lennox.

The piano in the hall stopped thundering. A few seconds later Mrs Wilson came back. She wasn't angry any more.

"If I put on a yellow wig and sunglasses, would everyone think I was Wayne Stag?" she asked. They all giggled.

There was a knock at the door.

"Come in if you are famous and can open the Fete," called Mrs Wilson.

In walked Crystal Cummings. She was wearing a new blue dress. She was smiling, and looking forward to running the Book Stall.

"I've come to collect your old paperbacks, Mrs Wilson," she said. "Isn't Wayne Thing coming after all? Mind you, Mrs Wilson, that programme is rubbish. I never watch it."

"Really?" said Mrs Wilson and Miss Mopper together. They watched 'Dean Street Diary' every Tuesday, Wednesday and Friday at eight o'clock, even if they had to finish their school work afterwards.

"Why don't you ask the Mayor to open it?" said Crystal.

"He's on holiday. I saw it in the paper," said Miss Mopper.

"The Queen?" said Lennox. "Me?"

Mrs Wilson rubbed her forehead. "Wayne Stag isn't coming, but one of my horrible headaches is," she said.

Nobody could think what to do. Mrs Wilson, Miss Mopper, Michael, Lennox and Crystal all stared glumly through the window.

"All those people out there look so excited," said Lennox. "They are all waiting for the Fete Which Cannot Open."

Everybody in the playground was busy getting ready for two o'clock.

One of the fathers who lived in the flats opposite the school had hurried over with his ladder soon after Mr Duckbody fell. Now he was putting up the flags for him.

Mr Duckbody had perked up. He was staggering across the playground, carrying a blackboard for the Pin the Tail on the Donkey competition. He was looking over his shoulder at the father putting up the flags.

A little boy was walking across the playground the other way. He was carrying a fancy glass bowl. His eyes never left it.

In the glass bowl was a bright green wobbly jelly. It looked as if it had not set yet. The little boy's mother had made this jelly specially. It was for the Afternoon Tea Stall. She was going to sell green wobbly jelly with ice-cream or green wobbly jelly with strawberries.

The little boy's mother never did sell that jelly. Her little boy walked straight into Mr Duckbody's legs. The jelly flew up in the air and landed BLURP! on Mr Duckbody's shoulder. It sat there like a thing from outer space.

Then bits of green began to slide down his blue shirt.

The little boy took one look and ran off back to his mum crying and clutching the empty bowl.

4

The Walrus and the Jelly

"Well, at least the bowl didn't break," said Miss Mopper.

No one else said a word.

They watched Mr Duckbody put down the blackboard. He walked slowly over to Mrs Wilson's window. He stood there, looking through at them.

Mrs Wilson opened the window. Mr Duckbody still did not speak.

"He's so unhappy," said Crystal.

Green jelly dripped down his shirt and onto his trousers. It was getting runnier and runnier. Mr Duckbody must have been very warm to melt the jelly so quickly, thought Lennox.

He sighed. He looked down and flicked a piece of jelly off his chest. It landed on Mrs Wilson's arm but nobody laughed.

"It doesn't matter," said Mr Duckbody. "It doesn't matter about the jelly. I've got paint all over this shirt already, you see. Paint from cleaning that photograph."

The ends of Mr Duckbody's moustache drooped right down to his chin. He sighed like the wind in an empty house and the papers on Mrs Wilson's desk fluttered.

"This isn't a Fete," went on Mr Duckbody. "It's a bad dream. It's a nightmare about sticky paint, broken ladders, dirty dogs and flying jelly. And that's not all. I haven't got any coconuts."

"How dreadful," said Miss Mopper.

"My mate from the market was going to bring them at twelve o'clock. Where are they, may I ask? How can I have a Coconut Shy without any coconuts? And the stands have disappeared. I put them ready in the corner of the playground. Now they've gone. They're not even mine. They belong to another mate of mine who does charity work."

"We'll find them," said Miss Mopper, soothingly.

"I suppose I had better go and get changed," said Mr Duckbody. He tried to laugh. "Green just isn't my colour. So I'll get changed for the last time."

"Last time, Mr Duckbody?" said Michael.

"You might get covered in something else."

"I meant the last time at a Summer Fete. This will be the last time I am a Schoolkeeper here. All they do is mess me about. They can't even send me a ladder. I don't want to be a Schoolkeeper any more. At least you don't get covered with jelly on the dole. I've got my hobby. I'll put everything into that instead of into my job."

He wandered away.

"If he leaves, Mr Nobody will be our Schoolkeeper, not Mr Duckbody," said Lennox.

"Poor Mr Duckbody," said Michael. "He makes me feel like crying."

"He doesn't make me feel like crying," said Mrs Wilson. "He makes me cross. Moan Moan Moan. He has threatened to leave before. And what hobby is he talking about ?"

"I think he really will leave this time," said Miss Mopper. "He looks very unhappy."

"Like a walrus without any fish," said Lennox.

"Now then, Lennox, I think you should be more sympathetic," said Miss Mopper. "Mr Duckbody has had a rotten day."

"No Wayne Stag and now no Mr Duckbody," said Mrs Wilson. "What can I do? Perhaps I should run away. But Headteachers never do."

It seemed as if the whole afternoon was spoiled.

Then Crystal said quietly, "I have an idea."

"It's about time somebody did," said Mrs Wilson.

"Mr Duckbody had to get changed because he is covered in paint and green jelly," said Crystal. "He is so unhappy. We could cheer him up. Let's ask him to put on his best clothes and open the Fete."

"But Mr Duckbody isn't famous!" squawked Lennox.

"Why shouldn't he be famous just for one afternoon?" said Crystal. "He's much nicer than Wayne Whatsit. And you never know what people can do until they try." She smiled mysteriously.

"What an extraordinary child you are, Crystal," said Mrs Wilson. "I knew that the first day you arrived in the Infants and wanted to look at encyclopedias instead of playing with the plasticine."

"It's a brilliant idea," said Miss Mopper. "Instead of losing Wayne Stag and Mr Duckbody, we get them both in one. If you see what I mean. Of course, he may say no."

"He wouldn't dare say no to me," roared Mrs Wilson. She kicked off her comfortable old sandals and crammed her feet into a pair of brand-new shiny black shoes she had bought that very morning.

"Ow!" cried Mrs Wilson.

Then she put her head down and charged off after Mr Duckbody.

It was two minutes to two.

5

Why Are We Waiting?

At two minutes past two, Michael, Lennox, Crystal and Miss Mopper were waiting at the Cake Stall with Maria and Alastair.

They knew it was two minutes past two because Alastair kept looking at his watch. He wanted to eat his strawberry tart.

The others stared at the little stage with the microphone and hoped that someone would step up there soon.

Lennox clutched the tin with the change for the Bingo in one hand and his mother's red boots in the other.

"Don't forget to put them on again at half-past three when they judge the Fancy Dress," said Miss Mopper. "I'm sure Duke would never be seen wearing sticking plaster."

Michael's little sister Annie ran over to them. Her Bumble Bee face was smudged and one of her net curtain wings was torn.

"Give me the face paints and I'll make you

up again," said Michael.

"I finished them," said Annie.

"Oh no," said Michael. He imagined ears on everything.

"Michael is Superman," Annie told Miss Mopper proudly.

"Is he really, Annie?" laughed Miss Mopper.

"Yes. And Lennox is a funny lady."

"I am not. I'm Duke, the Cool Dude," scowled Lennox.

"I wish it would start," cried Alastair. "I want my cake! Lenny has had his lunch. I found him a big fat worm in the flower bed."

"Who made the strawberry tarts, Maria?" asked Crystal.

"I don't know, and I wish everybody would stop asking me. And be quiet about eating worms, Alastair."

"The Queen of Hearts made the strawberry tarts," said Lennox.

"No, she made jam ones," said Alastair.

"How do you know? It doesn't say what kind she made," said Lennox. "Perhaps he made them." He pointed to a little man with a sack over his shoulder. The little man looked

like one of the seven dwarves. He tottered over to them, and put down his sack.

"Have you seen the Schoolkeeper?" asked the little man. "I've got his coconuts here."

"Thank goodness, he was so worried about them," said Miss Mopper. "He's lost the stands as well. I suppose you don't know where they are, do you?"

"Sorry, ducks," said the little man. "I just couldn't get away from the market. That's why I'm late." He scuttled away.

"I wonder what will happen," said Miss Mopper. "Everyone is so tired of waiting. I don't like the look of the queue for the Jumble Sale."

The Jumble Sale was in the big hall. There was a long queue waiting for it to open. People were beginning to push and mutter that others had jumped the queue.

Miss Mopper could see Mr Grutt in the queue. Every Jumble Sale he complained if anything cost more than five pence, and said it was outrageous.

Miss Mopper could also see Freda Fogg. Freda Fogg always stuffed her plastic carrier bag full of jumble and then tried to dash out without paying.

"I'm glad Mr Jones is in charge of the Jumble Sale," said Miss Mopper. "I'm glad I'm in charge of Bingo, Books and Cakes."

"If Mrs Wilson doesn't do something soon, there will be a riot," said Crystal. "I think I'm going to go back and guard my books."

Everyone was restless.

The dogs waiting by the Pet Show began to bark and howl. The cats crouched crossly in their baskets. Mugwump crouched crossly and glared back at them. He wanted them to go.

Lenny the lizard stood quite still and did nothing.

An old man in the queue for the Jumble Sale waved his bag around his head and shouted "Socks! Long Johns! Socks!"

And around the Cake Stall ran Annie, shouting "Buzz! Buzz! Sting! Sting!"

Up marched a woman in a silky blue dress. Miss Mopper could see she was angry.

"Can't you sell me some cakes?" she shouted.

The blue silky dress had big padded shoulders like an American footballer. Miss Mopper was glad she had taken evening classes in self-defence.

"Er, I'm afraid we can't sell any cakes until the Fete is open," said Miss Mopper.

"It says on the posters it will open at two o'clock," shouted the woman. "It's late! And where is Wayne Stag? I've only come to see him. I'm going home. COME ON YOU LOT!" she shouted to her family.

"Oh please wait just a little longer," begged Miss Mopper. "I'm sure it won't be long now. And the parents and teachers have all worked so very hard to get everything ready. Just to make a little extra for the children. I know you'll stay—please?"

Miss Mopper smiled her sweetest smile.

The children knew she would win.

"Oh, all right," sniffed the woman. She shrugged her footballer's shoulders. "I suppose he's worth waiting for. You'll sell cakes as soon as it's open, won't you? I want some strawberry tarts."

"We'll sell them the minute the Fete is open," smiled Miss Mopper.

Suddenly the doors from the school burst open. Out charged Mrs Wilson in her shiny black shoes.

She clambered onto the little stage in the middle of the playground and tapped the

microphone to see if it was working. She smiled around at everyone, as if nothing had been wrong.

There was silence at last. Even Annie was quiet.

"Ladies and Gentlemen. Mums and Dads. Girls and Boys. Friends . . . "

"Lizards," whispered Alastair.

"I am SO sorry that you have had to wait so long," gushed Mrs Wilson. "Thank you all for being so patient. I have some bad news. Wayne Stag, who used to come to this school when he was called Wilfred Birkbottle, has forgotten us. I am afraid he is in Torremolinos instead. How could he forget his old school? How could he forget our wonderful children?"

There was a loud moan. Somebody blew a raspberry.

Somebody said "Wilfred Birkbottle? I remember him. He was horrible."

But lots of people started to move away.

"Wait!" cried Mrs Wilson. "Don't let him spoil our afternoon! We have some good news too. Somebody else is going to open our Fete. Ladies and Gentlemen, please give a good welcome to—THE COUNTRY COWBOY!"

Out from the school came a stranger.

6

The Cowboy and the Coconuts

The stranger wore a white suit with fringes down the sides of his trousers. There were shiny studs all over the jacket. He had high leather boots with spurs, and a big white hat.

"That man is wearing a stetson!" gasped Lennox. "He's a real cowboy."

As the tall man ambled nearer, they saw that he wore a turquoise silk shirt and a black bootlace tie. He carried a guitar.

"He's got a bow round his neck. It's Buffalo Bill. BUFFALO BILL HELLO," hollered Annie, jumping up and down.

One of the secondary school girls gave a loud wolf-whistle. The cowboy was very handsome! He stepped onto the little stage.

"Howdy, folks!" he drawled. "Ah am jest steppin in here to help this school. Ah will sing you a song, and it won't take long."

He didn't sound like a cowboy from the Wild West. He sounded as if he was from

Birmingham. But everybody was very quiet while the Country Cowboy sang his song into the microphone.

The song that he sang was beautiful! The children couldn't understand all the words because the cowboy's voice was all low and growly. He sounded like a bear from Birmingham. In the middle of the song the cowboy spoke instead of singing and it was all about being lonely in the mountains, with buffalos and baked beans.

Then he sang again and twanged his guitar.

When he had finished his song, the cowboy made a low bow and swept off his big white hat. Everyone clapped and cheered and stamped their feet.

The cowboy stood up again. He smiled and twiddled the ends of his long black moustache.

"Hey, I know him!" cried Maria. "It's—"

"Thank you, The Country Cowboy, better known to us as dear Mr Duckbody," cried Mrs Wilson, still clapping.

"Isn't he gorgeous?" said the woman with the footballer's shoulders. "I love Country and Western music. When is he on?"

"On?" frowned Miss Mopper.

"I mean, when is he on telly?"

"Oh. I don't know. I'll ask him," giggled Miss Mopper.

"Thankee, Mrs Wilson, Ma'am," drawled the Country Cowboy. "I name this ship—I mean, I declare this Fete OPEN. Spend all your money, folks. We need a tropical fish tank and a computer and all sorts of things to make the children really happy. And we need a new ladder most of all."

People rushed to buy things. They rushed at the Country Cowboy to get his autograph, too.

It was spend, spend, spend. The doors to the big hall were thrown open. The people in the Jumble Sale queue rushed in and tunnelled through the piles of clothes.

Lennox and Michael ran over to Crystal who was carefully setting out the books on her stall in alphabetical order.

"Crystal, did you know Mr Duckbody was a secret cowboy?" asked Lennox.

"Yes," she smiled. "At the end of last term I lost one of my stories somewhere out in the playground. Mr Duckbody found it and saved it for me all during the holidays. I told him it was my ambition to write thrillers. He told me his ambition was to be a Country and Western singer. Only he never dare sing to anyone. He used to sing in front of the mirror in his boiler room. He never told a soul until this afternoon."

"He will dare now, thanks to you, Crystal," said Miss Mopper. "Look. The reporter from the 'Haslington Gazette' is talking to him. He'll be famous."

"Hey! There are Mr Duckbody's stands for the coconuts," cried Michael. He pointed to the Plant Stall which had almost sold out. Now they could see that the two mothers had used Mr Duckbody's stands for their red geraniums.

People flocked to spend money on the Coconut Shy run by the Country Cowboy. Mrs Wilson, who was a good fast bowler, knocked three coconuts flying. She won back a bottle of sherry she had brought in as a prize. She gave it to the old man in the Jumble Sale because he couldn't find any Long Johns.

Mrs Wilson was very excited. The Fete was making lots of money. She would be able to buy three hundred rulers on Monday, *and* have lots of money left over for a fish tank and a new ladder. The computer would have to wait until next year.

At half-past three, Duke, Superman, the Bumble Bee and the others in Fancy Dress all got a prize. The judge was Mrs Canner the School Cook. She had baked doughnuts specially so that everyone could have a prize.

Alastair got a doughnut too, even though he had not entered. Mrs Canner thought he looked very exotic in his apron and tea-towel turban.

Lenny Lizard won a prize for the Best Behaved Pet.

Mr Duckbody was happy. He did not leave the school after all, and he started to sing at a Country and Western Club every Monday night.

Crystal was sold out of books, because she bought most of them herself.

The Cake Stall sold out quickly too.

But they never found out who made the strawberry tarts.